Behind the Chair

Behind the Chair

A GUIDE TO LIVING A JOYFUL AND POSITIVE LIFE

– Doll –

iUniverse, Inc.
Bloomington

Behind the Chair
A Guide to Living a Joyful and Positive Life

iUniverse books may be ordered through booksellers or by contacting:

iUniverse
1663 Liberty Drive
Bloomington, IN 47403
www.iuniverse.com
1-800-Authors (1-800-288-4677)

ISBN: 978-1-4759-6814-9 (sc)
ISBN: 978-1-4759-6815-6 (ebk)

Library of Congress Control Number: 2012923868

Printed in the United States of America

iUniverse rev. date: 12/17/2012

A Tribute to My Loving Mother

Even though you are gone
You will always live within my heart
For my heart smiles when I think about you
And all the joy and laughter that we've been through
Missing you more each day

Your loving daughter
Doll

Loving What You Do

Loving what you do
And making a positive difference within you
Makes life great, makes life fulfilled

Loving what you do
And enjoying each day that God grants you
Changes how you think and view others

Loving what you do

Contents

Chapter 1

Can We Live a Positive Life?

Can we live a positive life? Yes we can. Some ask me this even as they experience turmoil, gossip, and confusion. We must strive to live joyful, prosperous, successful lives—but, of course, it's up to you. You can either choose to be a caterpillar or rise above all the foolishness and strive to be a butterfly. I'm not saying that in the caterpillar stage of our lives it is easy. Life is not easy. We all make mistakes, but the learning process makes us stronger. We don't become that beautiful butterfly until we have gone through something, and that's what makes us humble and grateful. We all deserve to have a better life and good relationships and to live joyfully. We must pull each other up in our communities to be better human beings so that we all can benefit from everyone doing good. If we all are doing our best, we can help others do their best. The world would be a better place if we all were butterflies. So, don't stay a caterpillar; grow with me. The spiritual meaning of *butterfly* is an amazing transformation that takes place through Christ's redemption and regeneration when we are born again and become a new creation. "Therefore if anyone is in Christ, he is a new creation; the old is gone, the new has come!" (2 Corinthians 5:17 NIV).

> The past was my past, but now I want a better future. I will live my life for what it is rather than regretting it for what it is not. Living and loving life.

> It's easy to have a bad life, but you should strive harder to have a good life.

Even with all the ups and downs in life, always stay positive.

To go from a caterpillar to a butterfly is a blessing, and who does not want to grow better in life and have the ability to fly? God created this creature just like He created you. God has the perfect plan, and it is up to us to achieve it.

—Doll

"No one but you are responsible for your own life"
Oprah Winfrey

Chapter 2

Grateful

Woke up saying, "Thank you, God," for everything.
I woke up
The sunshine, even the rain
Water
Good health
My clothes
Shoes
My pets
Lights
Furniture
A job
Coworkers
Family
Friends
Money
Trees
Food to eat
Everything I come in contact with, I say, "Thank you, God;
I'm so grateful!"

Thank God for Jesus!

I am so grateful to be a hairstylist and to have traveled to some of the places in the world I have always dreamed of. Never in my wildest dreams would I have imagined riding a camel in Morocco in North Africa, seeing St. Petersburg Palace in Russia, being able to visit Iguazu Falls in Argentina, or seeing the flamenco dancers in Spain. I took a helicopter ride through the glaciers and went dogsledding in Alaska. I climbed in Ocho Rios in Jamaica. I even went to an ostrich farm in Curaçao, where I rode an ostrich that was running 50 mph.

My mom had passed away, so she was not alive to see history being made—the first black president, President Barack Obama. At the inauguration, I was in the crowd of excited, happy people who came from all over the world. I must say that was one of the best days of my life. I was so grateful to be able to vote and make a difference!

I am also so grateful to give back to the American Cancer Society. My salon collects wigs, hats, and scarves to make a difference in someone's life. I also walked for the All Shades of Pink Foundation, which helps men and women who are diagnosed with breast cancer. I am so grateful to be able to give back; being grateful means not just to receive but also to give.

Chapter 3

Back in the Day

When I was young, my mother had me in dance classes, modeling school, and singing lessons. I was always busy in different activities because my mom said I had a lot of energy and needed to put it to use doing positive things. When I became a teenager, my family had a band. I enjoyed being a part of that. But going out to the go-go and clubs was fun for me at that time. Jumping on stage, dancing, and even rapping gave me a chance to perform with the great, talented Chuck Brown. I was so honored to have that opportunity to be a part of go-go history. I enjoyed being onstage at the Capital Center to perform in front of thousands of people. I remember Chuck Brown chanting the words, "Whatever you do, big or small, do it well, or don't do it at all." I have also worked with Syke Dyke, a great and talented musician and producer from Trouble Funk who introduced me to Tee-Bone, who was a percussionist who trained me on the roller tons.

I went on to put out records. Some people said I was the first girl to do go-go. My name back in the day was Doll Baby. I had a song out entitled "So Delicious." I wrote plenty of songs and worked with lots of talented people in Washington, DC. I had a video that was on BET Home Jams.

I always loved modeling, and someone introduced me to Phil Collins. They said that he was a great photographer, and I felt really relaxed around him. I have been introduced to several photographers, and some made me feel uncomfortable when I was around them. When my mother was younger in the modeling industry, she had been raped by a photographer. I didn't want to be alone with a photographer without someone being there with me.

But the first time I did a shoot for Mr. Collins, I saw how professional and pleasant he was. The very first photo shoot we did was when I was Beauty of the Week in *Jet* magazine, December 4, 1989. I was a star for a week, and I signed so many copies of *Jet*. I saw my picture in barbershops, and I even got calls to visit the radio station. Because I had appeared in *Jet*, I was on the Donnie Simpson show when he was at the WPGC radio station. Also, I was in *Jet* on September 1, 1997; January 11, 1999; and December 27, 1999 (when I brought in the millennium New Year 2000). Now, as the four-time Jet Beauty of the Week, I had broken the record. After that I did several swimsuit calendars and other publications. I went on to cohost and host local television shows. Then I took classes at CTV 76 and became a certified producer.

I created *Doll's Beauty Show* back in 2000. While doing my show, I met positive people doing great things in our community. My cousin Richard Tyson was the videographer. He remembers my very first show when none of my guests showed up. I started crying and then wiped my tears and went out in the street and started interviewing people. The show turned out great after all. In the beginning days of *Doll's Beauty Show*, I used to edit and review all the shows until it became too much for me. I was trying to do everything, when I really needed to leave that to those who were better at those tasks. Michael Ray and Shelby Cox helped me out on a lot of the shows, and so did some of the students at CTV. We did over one hundred shows, including shows on CTV (channel 76) and DCTV. Also, I received over ten awards—some from CTV and DCTV.

While using all the gifts that God has given me, it helped me fulfill lots of my dreams. I jumped out of a plane at eleven thousand feet, was a clown in a circus, and rode an ostrich on the island of Curaçao. I even ate iguana soup. What I do for television! I watched Oprah Winfrey at 4:00 p.m. every day for years behind the chair. I always wanted to meet her or even produce a show for her. My mother always said pick the best role model, and I did—Oprah Winfrey. She had that go-get-it attitude, and if I had to look up to anyone, my choice would be the Queen of the Talk Show. Now she is the owner of the network OWN. She is a true example of how hard work does pay off.

Also, I looked up to Dorothy Height. She was the "Queen" of the civil rights movement. She sat onstage as Martin Luther King Jr. delivered his "I Have a Dream" speech, and she led the National Council for Negro Women for well over fifty years. I had the honor to have talked with her several times. I took a picture with her at her birthday party. It was amazing to be in the presence of a woman with style and class. I admired her fight for equal rights, and I would go every year to the black family reunion where I would see her. To be in her presence was an honor. Dorothy was a beautiful butterfly, and she will always be with me in my heart, forever missed.

> Without community service, we would not have a strong quality of life. It's important to the person who serves as well as the recipient. It's the way in which we ourselves grow and develop.
> —Dorothy Height (March 24, 1912-April 20, 2010)

> Never lose sight of your dream; work hard but never give up.
> —Doll

> Whatever you do, big or small, do it well, or don't do it at all.
> —Chuck Brown

> I believe you should use your ego for a higher good.
> —Oprah Winfrey

Chapter 4

Love What I Do

I love what I do so much! And it's not about the money. I have been doing public access television for over ten years—my show's name is *Doll's Beauty Show*. I filmed over one hundred shows for free. Even though CTV, channel 76, supplied me with their equipment, I had my own lights and camera. I went to CTV for classes and became a certified producer.

On my shows I had poets, fashion designers, entertainers, and even celebrities. What I admired most were my guests who were everyday, hardworking people in the community giving back. Those shows were so fulfilling and enjoyable. I would be invited to fashion shows where kids and adults would give to a foundation. I featured a schoolteacher who raised money for a student who could not pay her hospital bills so that we could help her mother. My show gave people in the community a way to be seen and heard. I loved the shows that featured people going through a devastating time in their life who just wanted to share their story to help someone else not give up hope.

I even traveled with my camera on vacation so people could see the world with me. I interviewed a trainer on exercise, and he said, "Just get up and get moving!" Like I always say, don't talk about it, be about it. Go get your dream! When you love what you do, it's not work—it's fun and exciting, and you have the passion and happiness you want to do it all day and night. During *Doll's Beauty Show* I met some of the most driven people in the community who worked regular jobs but found the time to do what they love.

You must listen to your heart and when your spirit says move, *move*! Follow your passion and do it in such a way that you can't stop until you finish with great results. Love your dream. Love God, and He will help you lead the way. You must stay positive, don't doubt, remain fearless, and press on. Do everything with *love*. Don't listen to the dream crushers. Stay focused on the end result, and remember: love what you do.

> If you can't figure out your purpose, figure out your passion. For your passion will lead you right into your purpose.
> —Bishop T. D. Jakes

> When you can do something without getting paid, you love it.
> —Doll

> It doesn't matter who you are, where you come from; the ability to triumph begins with you, always.

> What God intended for you goes far beyond anything you can imagine.
> —Oprah Winfrey

> Love what you do.
> —Doll

"Love What You Do"- Doll

Chapter 5

Miss Too-Blessed-to-Be-Stressed

Miss Too-Blessed-to-Be-Stressed came in the shop today, sad because her man has been cheating on her. They had planned to get married. He packed up and left her. He has no job and he has four babies by four different baby mamas. I never knew what she saw in him but it was none of my business. Let me start by saying the apartment she lives in is hers; she has a college degree and she has a good job. The car he was driving was hers. But she is crying, all upset over this guy who has a track record for hit 'em and quit 'em.

"But he loves me. Why is he leaving me?" she asks, crying out loud while I'm doing her hair. "What am I going to do without him? I can't live without him." She has everything in life going for her. But she wants to stress over the good-for-nothing boyfriend. "This is it! It is really over this time."

I said, "Yeah right, you said that before." She always lets him right back in her apartment. Miss Too-Blessed-to-Be-Stressed never learns.

> Surround yourself with only people who are going to lift you higher.
> —Oprah Winfrey

> Nothing can dim the light which shines from within.
> —Maya Angelou

> God is my provider, not man.
> —Doll

Chapter 6

Too Blessed to Be Stressed

Let me start by saying that I have been lied on, and I have been cussed out by someone who was supposed to be my friend who stole my clothes, jewelry, television set, and all my personal things. I've been cheated on and totally disrespected. I have had so many bills and credit card bills—there were times when I did not know how I was going to pay the mortgage. I remember sitting up crying all night long because I thought I was going to lose everything and be homeless. I would work, work, work, and still not have enough.

But, the biggest pain was to see my mother sick and suddenly pass away. That was one of the most devastating things to happen to me in my life. My mother and I were so close, and I loved her sooooo much! The Bible says to honor thy mother and father, and I did. I gave her all the love I had, and I gave her flowers while she was living. But the day came when she had to go be with the Lord. I knew God was in control.

So, when clients come in and start telling me their stories of how bad life is, I have to share some of my hard times. But I tell them this too shall pass. There is never a time that I can remember that I handled anything on my own. I always prayed about it and believed in God. I believe in staying positive and looking for the good in all the hurt and pain. I learn to let go and let God. I know deep down inside it is going to be all right. So, when you are going through something, meditate on the Word: "No weapon that is formed against thee shall prosper" (Isaiah 54:17 KJV). Keep reminding yourself that you are a victor not a victim. Knowing all the devil took from me, God will give me back and more. So I can say this to you because I can relate. You're too blessed to be stressed. Keep your head up, keep smiling. Don't look at the bad situation. Just know in your heart that the hurt and pain will change. Sometimes we have to go through tough times to make us stronger and to bring us closer to God. Thank God for the hard times too, because they make us appreciate what we have, and they will make us better people.

No one but you are responsible for your own life.
—Oprah Winfrey

Even after a storm, the sun always has to shine.
—Doll

Stress is caused by being here but wanting to be there.
—Eckhart Tolle, *The Power of Now*

I-Survived-It Checklist

- Financial hardships
- Being cheated on
- Sickness
- Being lied to
- Losing a loved one
- A car crash
- Mistreatment
- Losing a pet
- Losing a job
- Hurt
- Disappointment
- Disrespect

If I survived it, you can too! God may not come when you want him to, but he's right on time. You're too blessed to be stressed!

Chapter 7

I Live by Faith

I must start by saying I live by faith. When I go to work, I don't know if a client is going to walk through the door. Some days I have no one scheduled on my appointment book. Then ten clients come walking through the door. I can honestly say I rely on my faith in God to bring clients to me. On a spiritual level, we must believe and trust in God. Sometimes we worry over things that will never happen. But I remember when I bought my home, I said, "What if I lose my job or what if I get sick? But even if that happens, I have *faith* that God will make a way." You must have positive thoughts and put God's trust in everything.

Have you ever driven through a bad storm and could not see what was in front of you, but you trusted you could get home safe, and you did? You had faith. Your strong faith will see you through life's storms. When someone says, "Do you think I will make it through?" I always say, "Keep the faith." When someone says, "I'm broke; I have a lot of bills," I always say, "Keep the faith." When my client's loved ones are sick, I always say, "Keep the faith." The old saying states that it's not over until God says it's over. It's true. Being behind the chair doing what I love, I have had a lot of faith. But I know I would have not made it without God. I relied on God for everything. Sometimes we are tested in order to keep the faith. We must meditate on the Word of God because He is still in the miracle-working business. Sometimes it takes blood, sweat, and tears to be the person God wants us to be. I have belief and have faith and trust God for all things because God never fails.

The blood, sweat, and tears bring you closer to God. That is when you become a beautiful butterfly.

I never knew what God could do until I had faith and believed in God.

Miracles are possible when you have faith.

—Doll

Chapter 8

Be Fearless

Fear can and will control you if you don't shake it loose. When I was writing this book, thoughts in my mind said no one would read this book. No one is positive; they only like to read drama or sex books. But we know that's a lie. People need to feed the spirit with good things. It fills you up, makes you stronger, and gives you hope and purpose. My mother used to say, "Be careful who you listen to and look up to." We know listening to the wrong people can lead you in the wrong direction. Get rid of those old bad friends and move forward to a peaceful, blessed life.

Don't be scared of change because it's sometimes what's best for you. I've tried different foods, traveled to different places, and stepped out of the box—be fearless! Again, as I mentioned before, I've jumped out of a plane at eleven thousand feet, and I rode a camel, an elephant, and an ostrich. I've even petted a tiger and gotten into water with sharks; I've eaten grasshopper in Asia, iguana soup on the island of Curaçao, and bull-foot soup in Saint Thomas.

I know that people are scared of planes and eating certain foods, but you miss your blessings sometimes by living in fear. I'm not saying to do the crazy things that I have done, but step out in faith and try different things. Maybe it's a new hairstyle or something you would not normally wear. Enjoy new things—you never know; you might like change. Being fearless doesn't mean you want to die; you're not afraid to die because you trust God. Psalm 27:1 (KJV) says, "The LORD is my light and my salvation; whom shall I fear? the LORD is the strength of my life; of whom shall I be afraid?"

Don't be afraid of tomorrow; live for today.

—Doll

You gain strength, courage and confidence by every experience in which you really stop to look fear in the face. You must do the thing which you think you cannot.

—Eleanor Roosevelt

Pursue your dreams. If you fail, it is not because of fear.

Do not listen to fear; it does not have a voice.

—Doll

Faith is taking the first step even when you don't see the whole staircase.

—Martin Luther King Jr.

Chapter 9

Be Willing to Learn

Be willing to learn. You don't know it all. When I went to beauty school, I already knew how to shampoo. I had a part-time job shampooing in a hair salon. When I started hair school, I was ahead in a lot of things. My instructors would be teaching me, and I thought I was little miss know-it-all. Now that I train students, I know how important it is for a student to pay attention and listen. Most of all, they should be willing to learn. I find that stylists who grow in learning new styles, trends, and techniques make more money. Whatever field you're in, you must be willing to learn. Learn from the best. Watch the successful people doing what it is you love doing and then master it.

> Don't feel you know it all; be willing to learn.
>
> —Doll

> I hated every minute of training, but I said don't quit, suffer now and live the rest of your life as a champion.
>
> —Muhammad Ali

Chapter 10

Seniors-Gone-Wild—Forgiveness

I can't stand to hear people talking loudly on a cell phone. One of my clients (I call her Senior-Gone-Wild) is on the phone, fussing with her sister ever since that sister took a lottery ticket they both played together every day and cashed it in for herself. The other sister has been mad; she won't let it go at all. She says that her sister is a liar and a thief. She wants to know how her sister could be so evil. They used to come into the salon together, and we would have great conversations. But now if they come to the salon, you can feel the tension between the two of them. These seniors-gone-wild have big attitudes. They are rolling their eyes, making smart remarks, and just being bitter about the past.

I told them to let go of all the anger and heaviness that they are holding in their hearts. Believe it or not, they both go to church every Sunday, and they know the Word of God. But they are still not living it. To let money come between two sisters is nothing but the devil at work. The old saying that money is the root of all evil is true. It's a shame that two sisters arguing and wishing bad on each other is not of God. Money comes and goes, but love can last a lifetime. Colossians 3:13 (NIV) says, "Bear with each other and forgive whatever grievances you may have against one another. Forgive as the Lord forgave you."

God is love.

—Doll

Chapter 11

We Are All Winners in God's Eyes

We all are winners in God's eyes. *Doll's Beauty Show* has won a collection of awards over the years. My mother loved to see me getting all dolled up to receive them. But every time I won, I always felt that everybody in the room worked hard or just as hard as I did. I felt that they deserved them too. To hear my mom say, "I'm so proud of you," was why I went along with accepting them for her. But deep down inside, I knew that I didn't need a trophy or an award to justify who I am. If I want a trophy, I can go to the store and buy a trophy that says I'm the best.

But I think when you're a winner, sometimes it makes others who are not winners feel bad. So I stopped accepting trophies. I do my work because I love it, not for a title someone thinks I should have. My aunt used to quote that old saying, "If I don't get my reward here on earth, I'm sure going to get it in heaven." I know that everyone deserves to be acknowledged for their hard work, but sometime the ones who lose go on in life to be the winners. A title doesn't make me or break me. We are all winners in God's eyes.

> If you woke up breathing, congratulations! This is the best award you can win.
>
> —Doll

> I believe that every person is born with a talent.
>
> —Maya Angelou

Chapter 12

Thinking about My Mom

Today I got up missing my mom, thinking about, if she was here, what I would make her for breakfast or how I would brush and comb her hair. When my mother became a senior, I started to do things for her that she did for me when I was a baby. I would give her a bath and change her clothes. The times when her legs would bother her, I would push her in a wheelchair. There is not a day I don't miss my best friend. We prayed together in the mornings, then off to work.

I was at work when a walk-in came in, meaning this was the first time I did this client's hair. She was a young teenage girl—let's call her "Little Miss Smelling-Herself." Her mom sent her with a certain amount of money to get her hair done. But she wanted relaxer, color, and cut weave—the big adult package. So I told her that she didn't have enough money for that. She asked her mother if she could still get it anyway, and the mother said no. But she insisted on telling her mom that Boo Boo at school had her hair like that, and her mother paid for it.

With a stinky, funky attitude, she said to her mother, "That's why I can't stand you." She said to me, "She makes me sick." My eyes got big while the mother was just quietly, not saying nothing. She kept pleading to her mom, "Why can't I have the weave?" Her mother said, "You are too young." Then the girl started mumbling and rolling her eyes.

Now, would you believe that the mother said to go ahead and give her what she wanted? I was trying to tell her that she didn't need a weave. But the mother said to do it. They got the hair, and the girl snatched the hair out of her mother's hands and told me, "Here, put this in." She did not once thank her mother—just all nasty attitude.

As I did her hair, I told her how blessed she was since some mothers don't take their kids to get their hair done unless it's a special occasion. I said that her mother wanted her to come every week to keep her hair up. I told her how my mother was not living and how I appreciated my mother and respected her and would never talk to my mother in that way. I even asked, "What if she was not here, what would you do?" She would be looking nappy for sure.

Maybe she did not get all I was saying in the first visit, but as she kept coming back every week, I noticed a change. She was spoiled, and she was breaking out of those bad ways. I let her know that no one on this earth is going to do for you and give you that love like your parent will and to please respect and appreciate her mother. She got a summer job, and I suggested she pay for her mom to get her hair done. So her mom came and sat down and put herself first for a change.

> If you don't like something, change it. Change your attitude.
> —Maya Angelou

> A good thing to remember is somebody's got it a lot worse than we do.
> —Joel Osteen

Chapter 13

God's Love Is the Best Love

Because God's love is better than any love . . .

> I don't need a thousand-dollar shopping spree to feel good.
> I don't need a chocolate cake with all the toppings.
> I don't need diamonds, silver, gold, or a fancy big car.
> I don't need a man to tell me I'm beautiful.
> I don't have to be thin or pretty.
> I don't have to hang with the in crowd to fit in.

God's love means you're never alone. You can trust God's love. God is good; God never fails. He is peace, joy, and happiness. Most of all, God's love is powerful; his love will pour into your heart and then flow into others. I believe God blesses us so that we can bless others. God can use anyone to bless others. Do something today to show God's love in you.

Isaiah 43:18 says, "Do not remember the former things, nor consider the things of old. Behold, I will do a new thing, now it shall spring forth" (NKJV). My pastor, Pastor Strong, preached on that one Sunday, and it was life changing because those words in the Bible mean to stay focused and don't look back—walk in God's love. Another life-changing message came from Minister Yvette Gandy when she said, "Don't give up! Where is your faith?" There's nothing like hearing an inspirational message that changes the way you look at life. Through life's ups and downs, it always reminds me that God is in control!

There is no greater love than God. God is number one.

Jesus is nothing but the truth.

—Doll

God will do for us what we won't do for ourselves.

—Minister Yvette Gandy

I'm predestined for greatness. I can do all things through Christ Jesus who strengthens me. You are in your season of blessings, keep fighting the good fight.
—Carolyn Taylor, Lovely Ladies

Chapter 14

Dealing with Difficult Clients

In over twenty-five years of doing hair, things have not always been peaches and cream or good sailing. Now, I have had my share of difficult clients. Some come in with attitudes. Maybe something happened at work or their man was not treating them right. I don't know what is going on in their personal lives, but I know they're not happy when they first walk through the door.

One time, Miss Tinker Bell walked in, and I said, "Hi, how are you?" She said, "I'm all right," in a snappy tone. So then I asked her what she would like to have done. She pointed at a style in a hair book, and I said that her hair was not long enough. I suggested a weave, but she did not have enough money. So she said to do her hair, and I did. I put her under the dryer with rollers. She complained that it was hot, and then she said it was taking her hair too long to dry. Every time I checked it, her hair was still wet. After all of that, I styled her hair and gave her the mirror. Then she said she did not like it. But I had told her the style was too short for the style she really wanted in the very beginning. Her hair couldn't get that style without a hair weave. She said that she wanted it like the picture. I said again that her hair was not long enough for that style. Then she said, "I can't go out tonight looking like this." I had a shop full of clients, and they were saying how much they liked her own hair and that it looked nice. Then she grabbed my comb out of my hand and started combing it, messing her style all up.

So, staying professional, I let the drama queen have her way. I asked her to please let me curl it again. Then she said curl this, and I curled it. She said to curl this, so I curled it some more. I did whatever I could to please her.

Then she told me her hairstylist would not have done it this way. I was at my boiling point. *Hot!* I was in the caterpillar stage of my life, meaning in my earlier years of doing hair. I said, "Why didn't you go to your stylist then?" Then she said, "I came to you, but you don't know what you're doing." That's when I snatched the cape off and told her to get stepping! I had other clients waiting, so she got loud and we fussed back and forth. I picked up the hot, smoking curling irons and waved them in her face. I told her she better leave before she got burned. Then she ran out the door and called me a _____. I said, "Takes one to know one!"

Now I have come a long way, and I know that is not how you handle a difficult client. God has truly taught me patience. Plenty of days I had to go into the bathroom and pray. I have learned to bite my tongue and not spit fire. Now I handle the situations better, using these methods.

1. Don't have shouting matches.
2. If your client is loud, let her know in a soft tone: "I'm not yelling at you; I'm talking in a soft one."
3. Let your client know, "I'm trying to please you."
4. Try to have your client leave satisfied. You might have to redo the style, but make your client feel appreciated.
5. Do not wave hot curling irons in your client's face.
6. Do not argue with your client and definitely don't call her a _____.

Sometimes the money is not worth the trouble.

Treat people how you want to be treated.

—Doll

Chapter 15

Complaining

Have you ever met someone and asked them how they were and they gave you the whole rundown? They said, "My head hurts," or, "My back hurts," and they had something negative to say about everyone they had come in contact with. By the time you finished talking to them, you were sick. They were so heavy with their issues that they made you feel heavy too. I call these people "blood-sucking vampires." They will suck all the blood out of you and drain you dry until you have no energy left. I thank God for caller ID because when I see their number pop up, I don't answer it or I'm really short with them and I will tell them I'll call back.

Now working in the salon, the vampires do show up. I could say it's a beautiful day, and they would say, "Think it's going to storm." It's like they look for bad in everything. If they have a job, they complain about that. They punish everyone for how miserable they are—those blood-sucking vampires.

Complaining is not going to change anything, so to grow out of the caterpillar stage, you must learn how to be grateful. When you see good in everything is when you become a butterfly. You can take a bad situation and turn it into something good. I am grateful for health and life, and you should be able to thank God in the worst situation. See the blessing in any situation. Stop talking about how bad it is, and look at all the good. Now I believe the more negatively you talk, the more negativity you bring to you. The more you speak happiness and joy, the more you receive. It's a true fact. The good energy you put out, you get back. The bad energy you put out, you get back. So stop complaining before no one wants to be around you.

I had a flood in my basement. I could have fallen apart, broken down, and started complaining about my situation since my floors got destroyed and my furniture got messed up. But, my insurance got me all new floors and furniture that was better than what I had. A blessing came out of a bad situation. If a makeup artist applies too much makeup, just wash it off and start again, but stop complaining. If you are in a situation and you want to start complaining, think of something good, like the roof over your head, or that you woke up this morning, or that you have eyes to read this book. Just deal with the situation as positively as you can. I even try to see the good in people. Sometimes people tell me how bad a person is, and I still try to see the good in that person. But if you find that that person is really negative, then it's time to let go! I've always felt that complaining was a bad spirit. Just be happy to be alive!

> The energy you put out, you get back either way—bad or good.
>
> —Doll

Chapter 16

It's Girls' Night Out

It was girls' night out, and Sweet Pea and I decided we were tired and we needed to go home. The shop was really busy, and we needed to get ready for the next day because we both had early appointments—no club for us tonight. All we could hear were the girls in the shop talking about the club, getting their hair and nails done, putting on lashes, and going to the mall to buy their freak 'em dresses and five-inch heels. Cayenne Pepper and Poo Poo were already getting their party started with their drinks in cups, and they were not even at the club yet. They walked out of the salon on their way to the club.

The next day in the shop, some of the girls could not wait to talk about how drunk Cayenne Pepper was the previous night. Poo Poo, her girl, was saying Cayenne Pepper was sending her margaritas back because they were too weak. Cayenne Pepper started yelling at the bartender and even was arguing with some girls. Poo Poo said she was going to give Cayenne Pepper a ride home after the club, but saw her stumble out of the club and get in the car with Sweet Pea's man. Sweet Pea said he was at home. Poo Poo said, "Why would I lie? She drove off with your man, Cayenne Pepper." Sweet Pea got on FB and asked her man, "Did you give Cayenne Pepper a ride home last night from the club?" He replied, "No, I did not give that trick a ride." Then Cayenne Pepper said, "You need to stop lying; that's not all you did. Don't make me tell her the truth about what happened last night." Then Sweet Pea said, "Wait until you get to work. I'm gonna beat your _____."

Still not wanting to admit the truth and holding on to his lies, Cayenne Pepper walked into the salon. Everybody was watching because the personal business was all on FB. Sweet Pea jumped in Cayenne Pepper's face and said, "You tell me what happened." Cayenne Pepper pushed Sweet Pea on her face, then the next thing you know, they were fighting and pulling hair weaves all onto the floor. Sweet Pea pulled out patches. Salon rollers were all on the floor, and they were biting, scratching, and rolling all over the floor until the po po arrived at the salon and took them both away. Eventually the truth came out. Sweet Pea's man did have sex with Cayenne Pepper because they both were drunk; they blamed it on the alcohol.

Never discuss your personal business at work or on FB.
Don't get drunk hanging out with coworkers.
Your man should tell you if he gives your girlfriend a ride home.
Honesty and trust are very important in a relationship.
Do not bring personal problems to work; leave them at the door.

—Doll

Chapter 17

You Are Important; God Loves You

Never feel like you're not deserving of love, happiness, and money. Sometimes we get so busy with life, and we don't love ourselves. I have to take time to enjoy walks in the park, fresh air, and quiet time to get back to God's beauty. I relax, think of nothing, and clear my mind of thoughts, or I focus on how great God is. I enjoy taking baths to relax, listening to the water, and sitting outside, listening to the birds where I am at peace with God.

I make myself feel appreciated by buying myself flowers or something I want. If it's a diamond ring, I will not wait for a man to give it to me; I buy it myself. I don't wait for a friend to take me on vacation; I take myself. Don't wait for anyone to love you. Love yourself! Sometimes a bad relationship teaches us how to love. And be open to love! And care for yourself. It is not selfish to love yourself enough to not allow people to walk all over you and abuse you. Some people will take you for granted and get mad at you when you do not allow them to use you. Listen, I have been there when everyone came before me; I wanted to be liked, and I did not know how to say no because I did not want to hurt their feelings. Try saying no—sometimes it feels good. I have learned to love myself. I put myself first. I look in the mirror and kiss myself and know I deserve the best that life has to offer. "Love never fails" (1 Corinthians 13:8 NIV).

> You deserve respect, happiness, and true love—pray for it and don't settle for less.
>
> Don't settle for anyone treating you badly.
>
> —Doll

Chapter 18

Ride-or-Die Chick

All types of women get their hair done—from teachers to nurses to nine-to-five, hardworking people. But we also do hair for strippers, prostitutes, and drug-dealer girlfriends. Let me tell you about Miss Ride-or-Die Chick. She was a drug dealer's girlfriend. When you saw her, she was always wearing the best designer handbags—real ones. She had diamonds, bling, and the most expensive shoes. She was fly—meaning, girlfriend had it going on. She would pick out the most expensive hair in my shop. So when I got through doing her hair, everybody would be like, "Wow, her hair really looks nice." She and her man were always traveling and driving top-of-the-line luxury vehicles. I must say, she was living large.

I had not seen her for a while. Then a client asked me if I had seen her on the news. I said no. They said she had gotten shot in the head, and they never found the killer. Her man got locked up for all the drugs they found on him. I said, "Wow." That was the price the Ride-or-Die Chick had paid for her designer bags, luxury cars, and living the glamorous life. Death was the price she paid for selling her soul to the devil.

> When you admire what someone has, you never know what they did to get it.

> Never sell your soul to the devil—it's a big price to pay.
>
> —Doll

Chapter 19

I Learned from My Older Clients

I always learn from my older clients; I call them the silver foxes. They have a lot of wisdom and knowledge about history and life, but I especially love some of their old sayings.

1. You reap what you sow.
2. Never let the right hand know what the left hand is doing.
3. Where is your faith?
4. Learn from people's mistakes.
5. Laughter is the best medicine.
6. Let bygones be bygones.
7. Live and let live.
8. Look on the bright side of things.
9. Love will find a way.
10. Let God fight your battles for you.

Life is what you make it.

—Grandma Moses

What comes with gray hair is wisdom.

—Doll

Chapter 20

Being a Good Servant

To be a good servant will give you a break in the hair business. Jesus was a good servant of God. I was always asked to be the manager. There is no application out here that I filled out to get a job. I worked in the mornings, I worked nights, I worked holidays, I worked anytime someone said they didn't want to work their shift. People would come in the salon and walk right past the manager and come straight to me to ask for advice. They said they thought I was the manager. Because I was a good servant, they asked me to be the manager. Having a good attitude, smiling, and also having respect for others will make a client come back.

After work one day, I went out with a client. Our server in a restaurant forgot to bring the silverware. My girlfriend replied that was life-and-death. I said, "What do you mean? She just forgot the silverware; it's no big deal." She said, "Yes it is. I'm a nurse, and on my job if I forget to bring the tools that the surgeon needs to operate, that person can die." I had never looked at it that way, but it is so true. In every job, you should carry it as if it's very important—asking your client how she feels, or if she would like something to read. You can ask, "I'm stepping out. Would you like me to bring you anything?" "How would you like to wear your hair?" Let your clients know that you're a good servant by pleasing them and letting them know that you care. When my clients are happy, I'm happy.

Remember when you are going through something hard and you wonder where God is, the teacher is always quiet during the test. Oh, be sure to taste your words before you spit them out.

Remember to have a pleasing personality and be a good servant.

A strong positive attitude will create more miracles than you could ever dream about.

A good attitude is going to bring more to your life.

—Doll

Chapter 21

Remember the Good Old Days

Remember the good old days.

1. Remember when you would get your hair pressed and curled and you would cry because you were tender-headed and whoever was doing your hair was heavy-handed?
2. Remember when you would get all dolled up for church with your spiral curls looking like Shirley Temple, pretty dress and hat, ruffle socks, patent-leather shoes, gloves, and pocketbook?
3. Remember when we hung our clothes on the clothesline outside? We would bring them in, and they would be fresh and clean.
4. Remember when the fire hydrant was the neighborhood pool?
5. Remember when men and women wore finger waves?
6. Remember when you used to roll your hair with a paper bag?
7. Remember when you would leave your doors and windows open?
8. Remember when there were hatboxes and wig stands?
9. Remember when you had black-and-white televisions and you would use a metal hanger as your antenna?
10. Remember when you had eight-tracks, records, and tapes?
11. Remember when your family ate and prayed together at the table and you had to say, "Yes, ma'am," and "No, sir," and you had to call them by their last name only—Mrs. Thomas or Mr. Thomas?
12. Remember when you could never cuss around an adult or a kid? You would never disrespect a teacher or a person of authority.

13. Remember when you would pull your coffee table back and do the *Soul Train* line?
14. Remember when the plastic on the furniture would get stuck to you?

Some of you are too young, but I just shared a little history. Some of you still pass down family values.

> I remember when we had prayer in school. They should have never taken that out.
>
> —Doll

Chapter 22

Speak Out: Get It off Your Chest

In the shop we have speak-out moments where we get things off our chests.

1. Why do those Republicans keep lying and saying negative things about our president every time we turn around?
2. Why can't the media show more positive news?
3. Why do the reality shows portray black women as being ghetto and angry, and then show the blondes as being dumb? We know that's not true!
4. Why get your nails and hair done when you can't keep your phone on?
5. Why come out to the mall like you just woke up with your pajamas and slippers on, with rollers in your hair?
6. Why keep having babies when you can't take care of the ones you have now?
7. Why do some women wear open-toe shoes when their toes hang over the shoes?
8. Why do some people have expensive cars and live in the projects?
9. Why keep your weave in too long when you know it looks like a hot mess?
10. Why all gold teeth?
11. Why does your underwear have to be showing? I don't need to see all that.
12. Why do you have your sound system on so loud that it can bust your eardrums?

13. Why use a whole bottle of gel on your hair?
14. Why do you loan people money when you know that they will not pay you back?
15. Why do people complain but don't vote?
16. Why don't people tell you there is lipstick on your teeth?
17. Why don't people use lotion on their feet when they look like they are kicking up powder?
18. Why do people take a shortcut with words when they text, knowing that they can't spell anyway?
19. Why do people ask me a question and then turn around and answer it?
20. Why don't people think before they talk, and why do they let stupid stuff come out of their mouths?
21. Why do people say they do hair but don't have licenses?

In the shop we let it all out! Speak out straight with no chaser. We talk about everything.

Get it off your chest!

Chapter 23

The Love for My Pets

We are all deserving of love, including our pets. The excitement I get from them when I come home, they are like angels. When my mother passed away, it was very hard to deal with her passing. You see, my pets gave me a reason to get up and live. Lady, my girl dog at that time, was small, but her bark was big. It was hard for me to get out of bed. I was sad and crying all the time, still grieving over my mother's passing. But Lady, in dog language, would say, "Get up! Take me out!" while barking and pulling on my blankets that were over my head. She would annoy me until I would get up. She would bring me her toy to throw it because she loved to play fetch. I would break down crying, and she would lick the tears off my face. She never gave up on me. Lady brought me so much joy and happiness even at a time of sadness.

For some it is hard to understand why I treat my pets like they are my kids. But I call them my doggie kids. My cat of sixteen years sits beside me when I pray, as if saying, "Don't forget about me." I pray for my pets when I pray for everyone else. Some call me the doggie mom because I truly treat my dogs like the kids I never had. I have my pets on all of my Christmas cards because they are my family. My pets also take pictures with Santa. I also give my pets birthday parties where my clients bring their pets and we celebrate their birthdays and sing "Happy Birthday" and have doggie cakes strictly for dogs. I love to take them to the nursing homes because they bring so much joy to the elderly. My pets Lucky and Lady even walked for the Cancer Foundation. They did a lot of great things for the community to bring smiles to people's faces in the community. On *Doll's Beauty Show,* my precious pets did a doggie makeover. Lady even modeled in a doggie polka-dot bikini at Laurel Pet Show.

I truly miss Lady and my cat Tibby. They have gone on to heaven with my mother, giving big love. My life would not be the same without my pets. Now I have a new joy; her name is Baby Love. She is spoiled rotten and is my fashionable little diva. With her colorful bows, she loves the camera, and I've never seen a dog pose like this one. My clients love the pictures of her in doggie outfits that I share with them. We love to share pictures and stories about our pets in the salon.

> If you have a hole in your heart for joy, buy a pet.
> God loves pets too.

—Doll

Chapter 24

Three Generations of Hair

I do hair for every occasion—family pictures, birthdays, graduations, proms, weddings, divorce court, funerals, travel, church, dates, parties, and job interviews. To be a part of people's special lives is a blessing. I really knew I touched a client's life when a dear client of mine passed away. I went to the funeral and saw my hairstyles through her life in the obituary. That was very touching and moving for me. I did the hair of the grandmother, mother, and daughter. I was a very big part of their lives. It was an honor to be a part of their family tree.

History and heritage could be seen as hairstyles changed over the years and as my client grew from a caterpillar into a beautiful butterfly. It's always great when my clients allow me to be a part of their journeys with my styles.

Chapter 25

Relationship Topics

Relationship topics! In the shop I have women crying in my chair not because of how their hair looks but because of how badly a man has abused them and mistreated them, always lying to them and disrespecting them. They will tell you their man came through the door at three in the morning, saying they were hanging out with the boys. In some cases, it's true, except when it's all the time and you have never met the boys. But my aunt used to say that there's nothing open after three in the morning but a pair of legs. Then you go out to dinner with them and you pray over your food, but they don't. But why, when the phone is ringing, do they keep getting up from the table? They can take you to a club, give you alcohol, and get you drunk and sick, but they cannot take you to church. They always want to break up with you around your birthday or Christmas because they are too cheap to buy you a gift.

But, player, your time is up. Women here at the salon stick together to let the other women know the games that men play. We are very aware that there are good men out there—good men who have date night once a week and will shower you with lots of love and are proud to introduce you to their mother and pray and go to church with you. Behind the chair, I have heard some of the worst stories dealing with men. But God can fix any relationship. God does not want you to be a punching bag, so remove yourself from a relationship that hurts you. If you need to, call the abuse hotline and please get help—don't continue to allow a man to hurt you. God is love and not confusion. Pain is of the devil. Please don't get it twisted. If God is all you have, then that is all you need. It's okay to be alone for your peace of mind.

God is love, not confusion, pain, and hurt.
Love yourself enough to treat yourself well.
Never feel you don't deserve the best.
A man who does not love God cannot love me.

—Doll

Chapter 26

Jealousy

Jealousy is one big, common topic we women deal with. I know I have had to deal with it from the time I was a little girl with long hair down my back. I had a mother who spoiled me and gave me so much love. As a child, I remember kids saying I had a lot of toys and I don't your mom loves you more than my mom does. I was confused at that age and didn't know what that really meant. They did not know at that age that material things are not love.

When I was a teenager, a girlfriend I thought was a friend was having problems with her mother. She would yell and fight with her mother, so her mother put her out. I felt sorry for her, so I let her stay with me, and my mother treated her like she was her daughter and cooked for her. And my mom bought her clothes when she bought me clothes. I came home one day to discover that my clothes, jewelry, shoes, and TV were gone. Let's say I was robbed, and she was nowhere to be found. I called the police and went to look for her at her mother's house. Her mother said she had found some things that look like mine. She then admitted to stealing my things and throwing some of them in the trash.

Jealousy will make you do some hateful, evil things. I took her to court, and she had to pay me in installments. But I learned then not to trust insecure, unhappy people. When people are happy about themselves, they can be happy for you. When they are not, watch out. They are like crabs in a bucket and will try to pull you down. I stay around people who lift me higher. I can pay a person a compliment because I'm secure about myself. I can help and give the best to those I love because I'm secure about myself. Jealousy does nothing but hurt a good friendship and will destroy you from being the great person God is calling you to be. Jealousy and evil are not of God. God is love.

> To be jealous of someone is not positive; it is negative.
> Don't be like crabs in a bucket.
> When you are happy about yourself, you can be happy for someone else.
>
> —Doll

Chapter 27

Be Yourself

Sometimes you are best off keeping things a secret. Well, I made a mistake and told my girlfriend where I shop. When we would go out shopping, she would pick up everything I picked up and would want to buy the same things I liked. If I bought a dress, she would buy the same one in the same color. I could not understand why someone would want to look exactly like me. God created us all to be different. We have our own dreams, style, and direction. We should have our own identity. I have a mole on my left lip that God blessed me with. Well, this friend of mine took a black pencil and drew a mole on her lip. That's when I thought it was really getting serious and I needed to talk to her.

I told her to please be herself. I thought it was flattering, but she needed to be herself. As much as I admire Oprah, I don't think she would wear some of the clothes I wear. I don't think Oprah would wear the leopard boots on this cover of the book or the wild colors I put on my nails. We don't even have the same pets. Unless you are a twin, there is no need to copy. Follow your own path and ask God for direction. We all have different gifts and talents. Every one of us is unique in God's eyes. There is only one President Obama, one Oprah, one Maya Angelou, and one Madame C. J. Walker—and God created one you! Find your purpose, follow your dreams, and be yourself—the person God wants you to be.

Live your best life.

—Oprah Winfrey

Be yourself; be unique and stand out.
Everyone has a purpose; find it.
Some people would love to walk in your shoes, but when their feet hurt, they want to take the shoes off.

—Doll

Chapter 28

Hair Tips by Doll

The ten most-asked hair questions:

1. What makes my hair grow? It's what you eat. Veggies are the best, also hair vitamins and good hair products.
2. Do I need to condition? Yes, it's very important. Deep-conditioning packs are good if you're conditioning at home, or ask your stylist to give you a deep-conditioning treatment. Once a week is good.
3. My hair looks dull. What can I do to make it shine? Try oil treatment or a clear semipermanent color.
4. Do I have to get my ends trimmed? Yes, it makes your style last longer. It's dead hair anyway, and eventually you will have to get it trimmed.
5. I have bad dandruff. What can I do? If it is not a lot, there are dandruff shampoos that are good. Some have T-Tree in them; they make your scalp tingle. If the tingling does not stop, it is best to be treated by a doctor.
6. What will cover my gray? If you have 70 percent gray, I suggest permanent hair color. If you don't have that much gray, then semipermanent hair color is a good choice.
7. What can I use for breakage? A protein treatment strengthens the hair and keeps it from breaking.
8. What is a good shampoo if my hair feels dry and brittle? Use a gentle shampoo with moisturizer in it.
9. How can I avoid my weave or my hair tangling up when I shampoo? Brush your hair out before you shampoo.

10. How do I maintain my style? Use a silk or satin scarf. Then wrap or roll your hair up at night. Avoid cotton pillowcases since these dry your hair out. You should regularly shampoo and condition your hair and keep it clean.

Chapter 29

Let's Celebrate the Living

Let's celebrate the living butterflies who go an extra mile every day to show love. You know the lady who smiles and says hi may hug you and tell you everything is going to be okay, and she takes time to listen when you want to talk. The teacher who spends time after school to tutor you. The nurse who takes extra care to make you feel better. The man or woman who showed up to save your life. The person in your life who is always there when you're down and out. Also, that person who may have given you his or her last money to help you pay a bill or get you out of a tough situation. Show them love and just thank them. They are the butterflies who fly around spreading love, while some are growing to get there. If you know that one special person, show the gratitude and appreciation you have for that person, because he or she doesn't have to be kind and caring. But they spread their beautiful wings and fly all around you with love and compassion. God's creatures stretch out their love more than a caterpillar because a caterpillar does not know love until it grows to God's magnificent creation. So when you see the person who gives more, thank him or her, please. Learn from those great people who serve our communities every day; strive to be like them. Let's grow together.

Chapter 30

Smile Challenge

Today I would love to challenge you with smiling all day. No matter if someone cuts you off while driving, or someone bumps into you and does not say excuse me, or someone close to you gives you bad news—when you walk in a room and smile, it brings good energy and fills a room with happiness. A smile is contagious and makes others want to smile too. People gravitate toward happy people, but no one wants to be around sad, depressing, negative people. People tell me all the time they love to be around me because I'm positive and happy about everything. I call it the joy of the Lord. Give God all the glory, even in the hard times. Hang on to your smile. Think of pleasant things.

I was a clown in the circus for one day filming *Doll's Beauty Show*, and I called myself the Happy Clown because I wanted to bring smiles to all the kids' faces, and that I did. When you want to smile, think back to things that make you smile. Think about a pet or your kids—something that makes you happy like cheesecake or ice cream. Try to keep your joy all day. Laughter is good for the spirit. Happiness is a feel-good medicine. So good luck with the smile challenge. What do you get if you smile all day and don't give in? A blessed wonderful day. Smile on!

> God smiled when you were born.
> When you walk in the room with a smile, you radiate good energy and make everyone want to be there.

> A smile is free.

> —Doll

Passion is energy. Feel the power that comes from focusing on
what excites you.

—Oprah Winfrey

Chapter 31

Giving Back Feels Good!

I want to be blessed to be a blessing in someone's life. That is why it is so important to give. It's a universal truth to give back. It not only makes the person you're giving to feel good, but it makes you feel good. It is very important to be a cheerful giver. When I think of a person who does not give, I think of a person who is robbing himself or herself of a blessing. Giving back on Sundays is great, and helping others to achieve their dreams and doing community service are great. Showing compassion will even bring out the best in you. It empowers others to have a better future. It's a personal fulfillment and the happiness you get from giving. It makes others want to do the same. There are so many volunteer programs to give back to, and so many organizations need help. Churches are always in need of good service. Start right now in your community.

I love to give

> thanks to God
> support
> back to the community
> a compliment
> my time
> a smile
> advice
> my honest opinion
> respect
> love and compassion

You have the power to change someone's life.

—Oprah Winfrey

It's all about love.
Keep spreading love all over the world.

—Doll

Chapter 32

Let's Keep Violence off of FB

Posting personal information on FB can mess up your reputation and even keep you from getting a job. Lots of employers look at what you post to see how you act off work. I've seen people post photos of themselves smoking weed, posing naked, and having arguments. I have deleted friends because of this. I have friends now who post positive, uplifting messages, and beautiful photos of their pets, kids, flowers, and spiritual messages. The love that I feel with the friends I have now is great. If your friends are not growing in the direction you're growing, delete those friends and move on.

You are growing from the caterpillar to a butterfly, which means you can't be a butterfly and hang with the caterpillar. In church we say you don't want to backslide by going back to those old ways. You have to let go of those folks doing those things you used to do, like doing drugs, smoking weed, drinking, cussing, and anything that is going to keep you from growing in the love of God. When you love God, you don't want to disappoint God. It's a process. Sometimes I've seen people grow slowly and some faster than others. It starts when you decide you love yourself enough to make a change in your life. Let's celebrate the ones willing to change. Encourage them, pray for them, and don't give up on them. Prayer does work. I witness it in my life.

Acknowledgments

Thank God for my father, mother, aunt, and family and friends encouraging me. They prayed for me. I have been saved several times, baptized twice. But I still was not ready to totally give my life to God until Minister Yvette Gandy came to my shop to get her hair done. She would take time out to pray with me and pray over my hands. She would place anointing oil over my hands and bless them. She prayed for me for over five years, and she kept inviting me to church where she would preach. I attended her church, and her testimony touched my heart. She is a true example of God's love. I kept attending her church and saw the change in my life. I love the praise and worship of giving God the glory for all the blessings. Pastor Strong is a great pastor, and he teaches the Bible in ways that are easy for me to understand. Seeing this man of God showing God's love is beautiful. The members welcomed me with open arms and showed me so much love. I decided to make City of Zion my church home.

I know my mother is smiling in heaven with the decision to be a butterfly. I chose this walk and I didn't do this for anybody but God. I decided to surrender and give myself to Christ; this does not mean I'm living a boring life. It means I'm living a better life. I'm excited to go to church and learn the Word of God and share it with everybody. It's a joy you can't imagine. It's better than any love any man can give. God's love is awesome and amazing. Thank You, God! Thank You, Jesus. Special thanks to Mr. Phil Collins (photographer) and Allison Gregory Daniels (consultant). I would also like to thank CTV (channel 76), DCTV, and MCTV. I appreciate the support of the staff at iUniverse, and I certainly want to thank dglSolutions and my Chelsea's Beauty Supply family.

Behind the Chair is dedicated to my mother who only wanted the best for me and who, like any mother, wanted to teach her child the ways of God and to never give up on oneself. I have the best clients in the world who support me and grow with me—we encourage each other. It's a sisterhood, not just a shop where you get your hair done, but a little shop of *love*!

Final Thoughts

I dedicated this book to my mother because I spent a lifetime wanting to make her proud of me by being a model in magazines, performing on stage, being on CDs, and being a manager of several salons. Now I am working for myself at Doll's Hair Studio and also having an award-winning local public access show, *Doll's Beauty Show*. Now I have written this book, *Behind the Chair*. All my mother really wanted me to be was a good person—that is it, that's all. It's the same thing that God wants you to be—a good person, living according to the Bible. Strive to be the person that God wants you to be and live the blessed life that you deserve.

In peace, love, and happiness, butterfly, you fly with your colors so vibrant and beautiful that everyone has to stop and admire God's beauty.

Jesus is my Lord and Savior.

Don't give up!

> When the caterpillar thought the world was over, it became a butterfly.
>
> —Unknown

Contact Information
Author and Writer
Doll
Website: www.dollsbeautyshow.com
E-mail address: doll@dollsbeautyshow.com

Phil Collins (Photographer)
Allison Daniels (Consultant)
www.AllisonGDaniels.com